Davina and the Dinosaurs

Written by Wes Magee
Illustrated by Tracy Fennell

Collins Educational

Leon was given six chocolate dinosaurs for his birthday.

They were wrapped in silver paper.

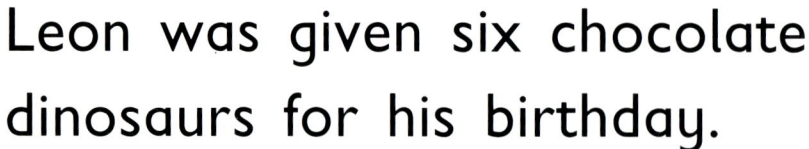

Leon stood the dinosaurs in a long line in his bedroom.

"One,
two,
three,
four,
five,
six!"

Just then his mum called him.
He ran downstairs to the kitchen,

and while he was away who should spot the dinosaurs but Davina. She was Leon's little sister.

Chocolate! Oh, yes!
She peeled the silver paper
off Stegosaurus and gobbled
up its leg. *Ummmmm!*

Then she peeled the silver paper off Brontosaurus and munched off its head. *Ummm! Yum!*

And then she peeled the silver paper off Tyrannosaurus Rex and bit off its tail. *Ummm! Yum! Yummy!*

Suddenly, Davina heard Leon coming upstairs. She grabbed the rest of the dinosaurs and ran away to hide.

Leon looked everywhere for his dinosaurs.
"Mum," he shouted, "my dinosaurs have gone!"
Mum came upstairs.

"Look!" she said, pointing to some silver paper on the floor.

Leon and his mum followed the trail of silver paper.

The trail led to Davina's bedroom.

And they found her hiding under the bed.

"Mum," cried Leon, "she's eaten *all* my dinosaurs!"

Davina had chocolate all over her hands. And she had chocolate all over her face.

"It wasn't me!" said Davina.